WE CA

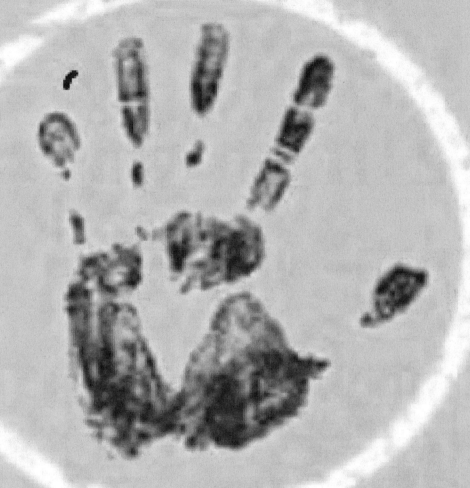

ERADICATE
RACISM

The United States of America is afflicted with a deep spiritual disorder

The tensions, divisions,
and injustices besetting
America are symptoms
of a long standing illness

manifest in rampant materialism, widespread moral decay, and a deeply ingrained **racial prejudice**

No one is immune to this
disorder, we are all
members of this society
and suffer the effects
of its maladies.

Subject to
systemic injustices,
millions
of Americans
are prevented from
making their full
contributions
to society and
partaking in
its benefits.

How do we create
a culture of inclusion
where we live in unity
within our multiplicity?

How do we honor our
diversity within our
common heritage
as human beings?

How do we safeguard our differences while recognizing we are more alike than unalike?

What will free us from attachment to inherited and unexamined assumptions?

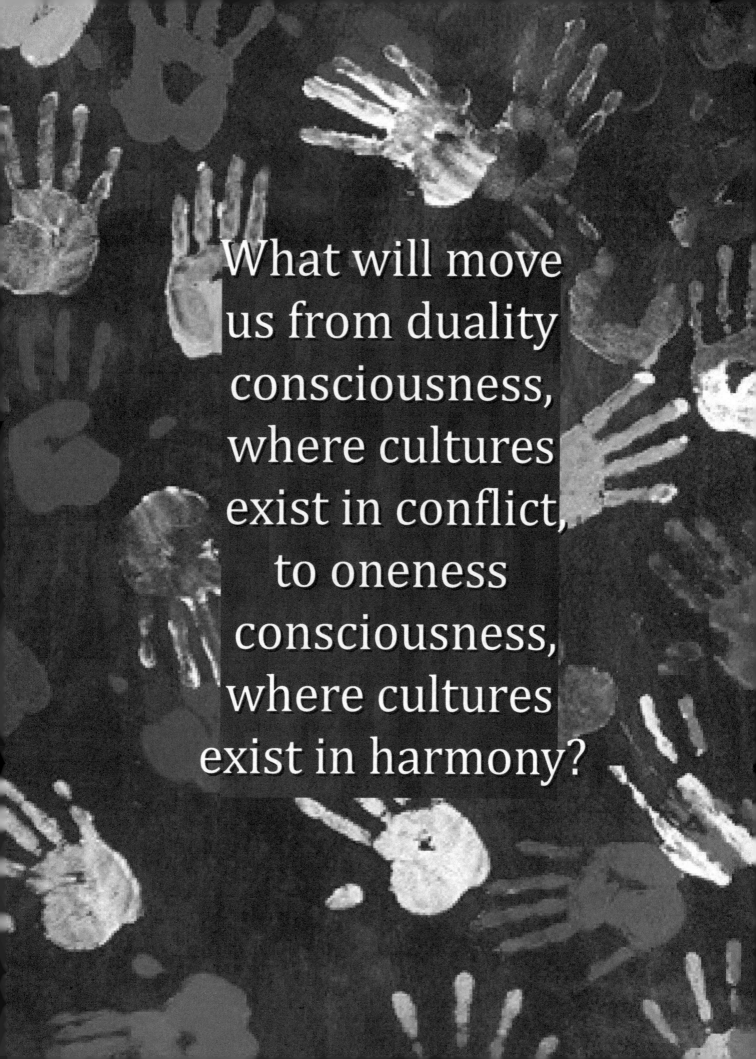

What will move us from duality consciousness, where cultures exist in conflict, to oneness consciousness, where cultures exist in harmony?

It is by
re-conceptualizing
the way we
approach
conflict
and
the way we
handle
life's
journey.

By
re-conceptualizing
the way we see
the world
and
understand reality.

By
re-conceptualizing
how we view
relationships
and
interpret
human identity

and,
most of all,
by
re-conceptualizing
the nature and purpose
of divinity.

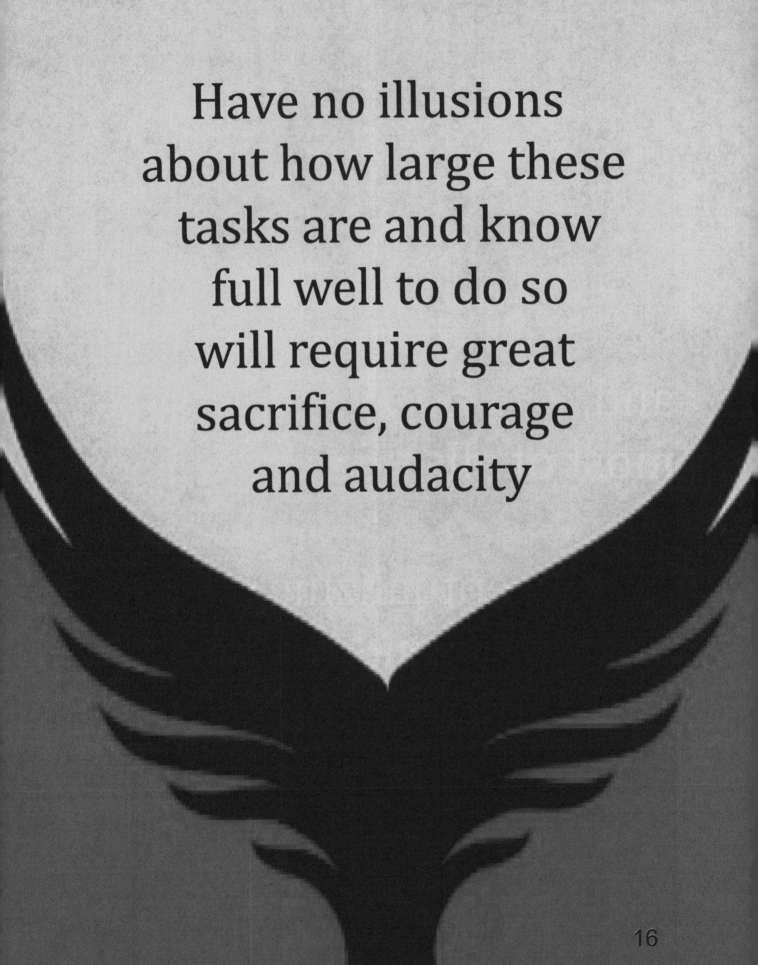

Have no illusions
about how large these
tasks are and know
full well to do so
will require great
sacrifice, courage
and audacity

However, these shifts have already begun to happen on a global scale at the grass roots level.

Faith communities, social justice organizations, and many others, are working on parallel paths to achieve the same end, bring into full awareness the <u>consciousness of inclusion.</u>

This transformation
is gaining momentum
and is renewing
the entire planet
by engaging the
hearts of people
everywhere.

After many millennia of
living in difficulty, dissension,
and discord, humanity is
now rediscovering a
deep seated desire to live
in this world as one.

A powerful example of this deep seated desire is the Women's March simultaneously taking place on seven continents.

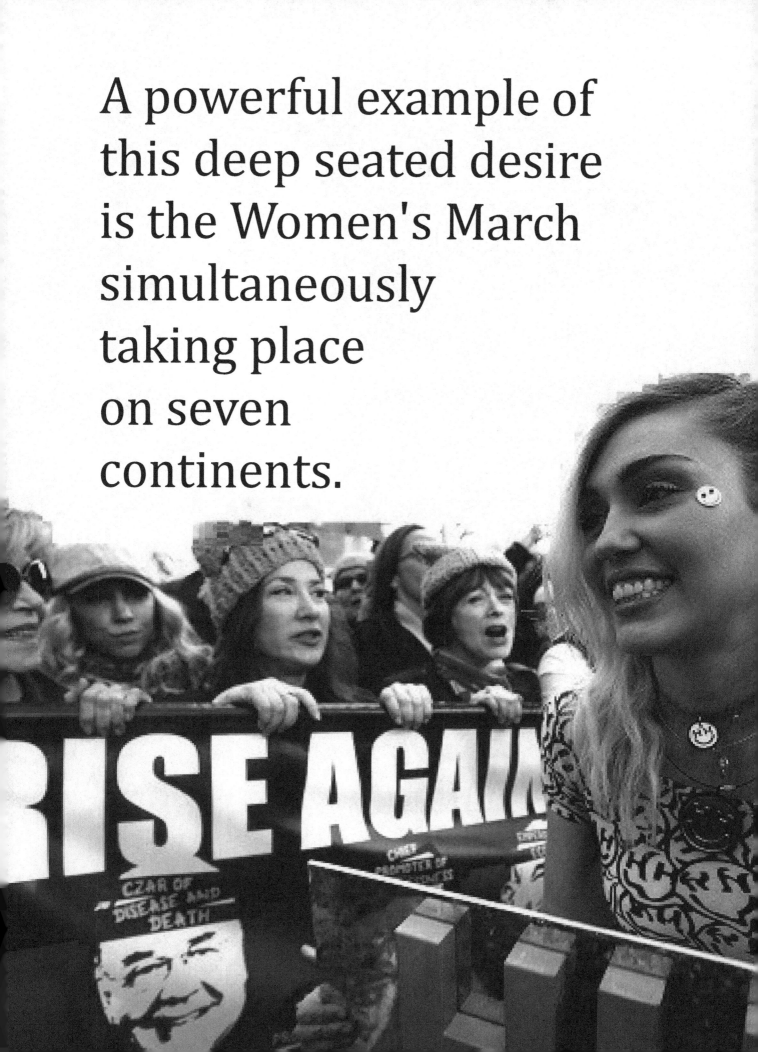

You can trace the genesis of this global desire to build a culture of inclusion back to the mid-19th century origin of the Bahá'í Faith.

Bahá'u'lláh has lent a fresh impulse and set a new direction to a two fold process now operating in the world.

On the one hand, we have the process of taking on the identity of world citizenship

On the
other hand,
the tribulations
present in the world
are the consequences
of mankind's failure
to recognize the
All-Knowing
Physician and
apply His
remedy.

Ironically, these afflictions are hastening the consummation of The Golden Age of Humanity promised in every religion

The conscience
of the world must be stirred
to precipitate a radical
change in the very
conception of society to
coalesce the disjointed,

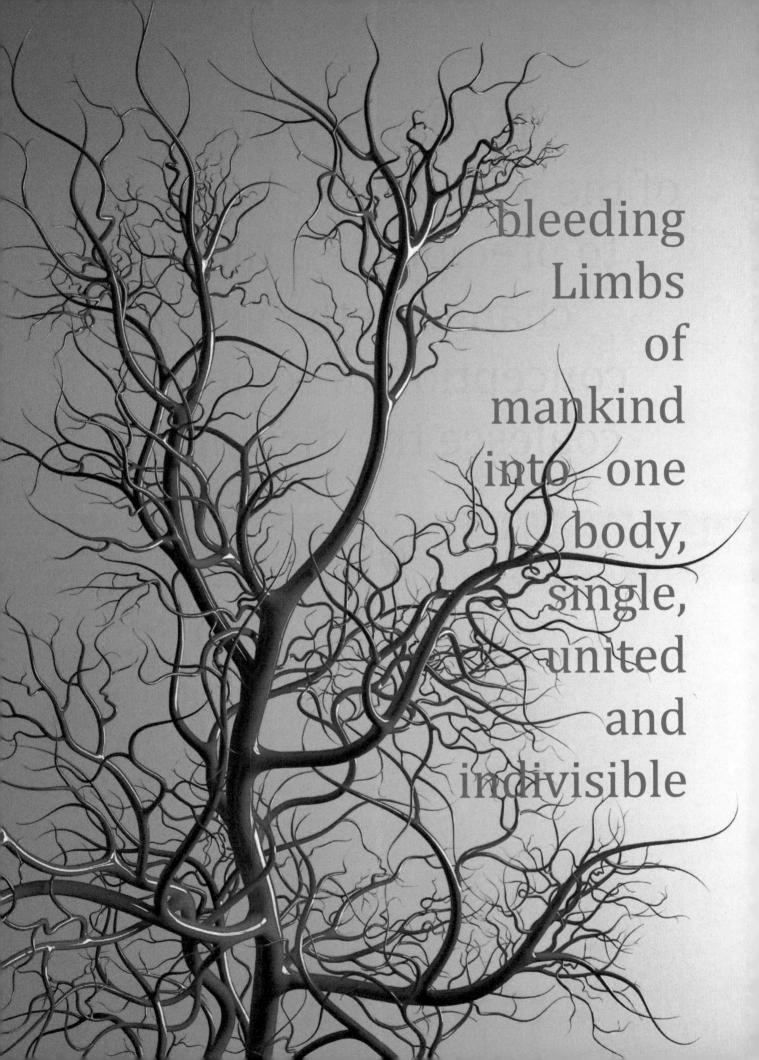

bleeding
Limbs
of
mankind
into one
body,
single,
united
and
indivisible

The resolution to these challenges lies in recognizing and embracing the truth at the heart of Bahá'u'lláh's Revelation, the incontrovertible truth **mankind is one.**

Ignorance of this truth is itself a form of oppression, for without it, it is impossible to build a truly just and peaceful world.

The Oneness of Mankind

is the center of a
supporting set of
interconnected
spiritual principles
all necessary to
achieve social justice
and world unity.
such as ....

gender equality

economic
equity

environmental
stewardship

racial
unity

(and more)

These principles represent the consummation of human evolution, an all-embracing vision of humanity's future.

The principle of
the Oneness of
Mankind,

the
pivot

round
which
all
Bahá'u'lláh's
teachings revolve,

is no mere outburst of ignorant emotionalism or an expression of vague and pious hope.

Its implications are deeper, its claims greater than any which the Prophets of old were allowed to advance.

Its message
concerns itself
primarily with
the nature
of the essential
relationships

that must
bind together
the nations as
members of
one human family.

The
principle of
the Oneness
of Mankind
carries
with it a
solemn
assertion.

The attainment
of the necessary
and inevitable
final stage in our
STUPENDOUS EVOLUTION!

We will slowly but surely take on the wider identity of world citizens.

Like all movements, this won't be completed overnight. Nothing short of a power born of God can succeed in establishing it.

OUR
CHALLENGE
IS TO DISREGARD
THE FLEETING NEGATIVE
NOTIONS OF TODAY

Instead, recognise their sharp contrast to the overriding spiritual forces of our time

These forces will compel us to put into action the principles the world needs for lasting collective security.

These forces will lead to the realization of a system of inclusion, incorporating global justice, equity, and unity in humanity's inevitable march toward world peace.

Bahá'u'lláh's laws and exhortations constitute an inseparable part of the foundation of such a society.

Bahá'u'lláh declares:
The object of every
Revelation is to effect a

TRANSFORMATION

in the whole
character of
mankind.

A TRANSFORMATION

that shall manifest itself both outwardly and inwardly and affect both its inner life and external conditions

Bahá'u'lláh's appearance signals the EMERGENCE of a race of men purified from the defilement of idle fancies and corrupt desires, the nature of which is inscrutable to all save God, who will manifest the signs of His sovereignty and might upon earth

The teachings of Bahá'u'lláh

*provide
such means as
lead to the elevation,
advancement,
education, protection
and regeneration
of the peoples of Earth.*

Enshrined in Bahá'u'lláh's Revelation is a pattern for a future society, radically different from any established in the past.

This final stage implies
ORGANIC CHANGE
in the structure of
present-day society,
a change such as the world
has not yet experienced
.

As the world now faces its most pressing challenges yet,

we acclaim Bahá'u'lláh as the

One Whose teachings will usher in the long promised time whenall humanity will live side by side in peace and unity.

From His early youth, Bahá'u'lláh was regarded by those who knew Him as bearing the imprint of destiny.

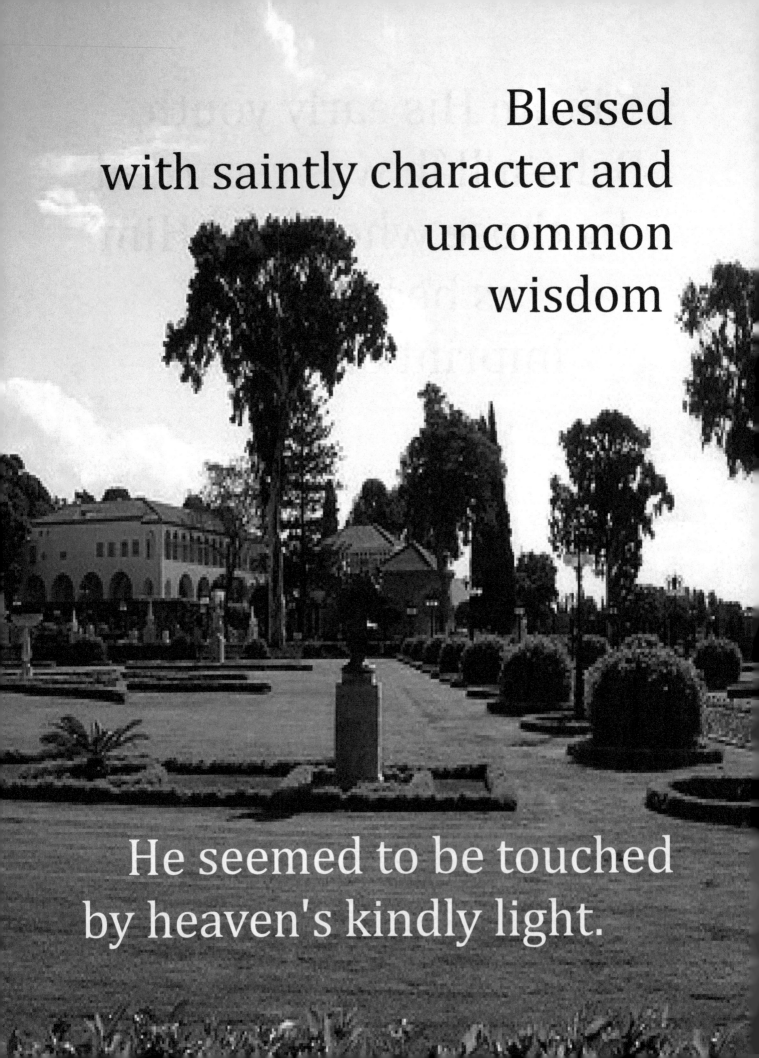

Blessed
with saintly character and
uncommon
wisdom

He seemed to be touched
by heaven's kindly light.

Yet
He was made to endure
forty years of suffering,
successive exiles
and incarcerations

campaigns
to vilify His name
and condemn His followers,

violence upon
His Person and
shameful attempts
on His life,

at the decree of two despotic monarchs.

All of which,
out of a boundless
love for humanity,

He bore willingly,

with
radiance,
forbearance
and compassion
for His tormentors.

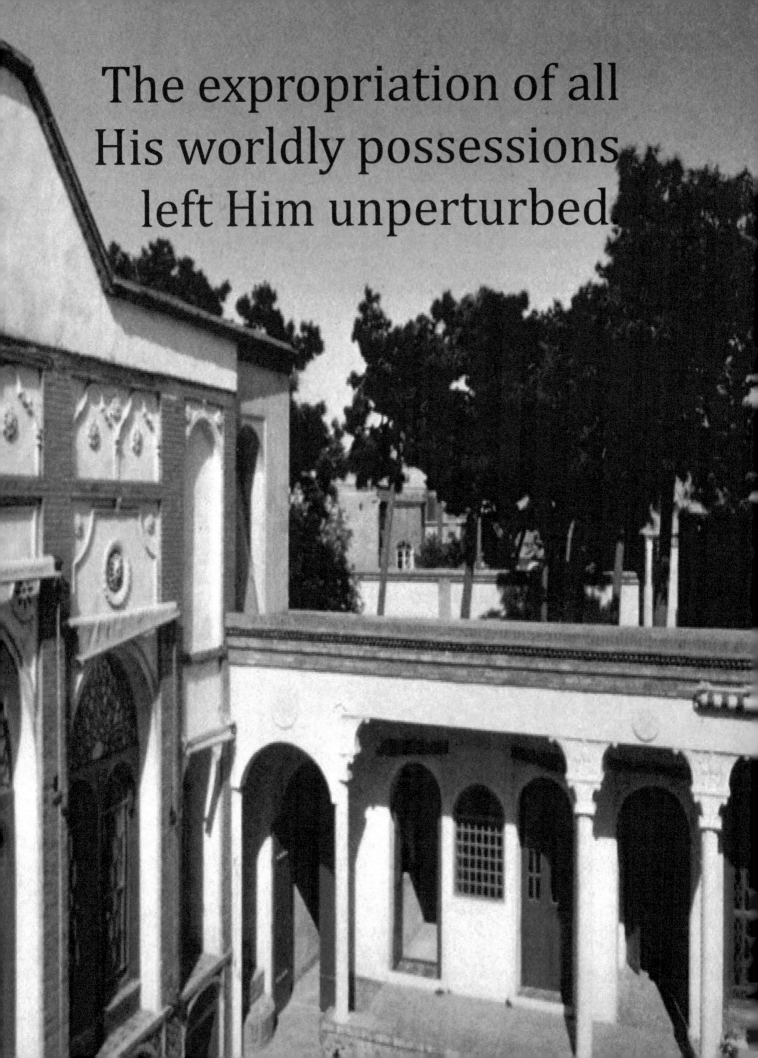

The expropriation of all
His worldly possessions
left Him unperturbed

An observer might wonder why One Whose love for others was so complete should have been made the target of such hostility,

given
He had
otherwise
been the
object of
universal
praise and
admiration.

Famed for His benevolence,
High-mindedness
and disavowing
any
claim to
political
power.

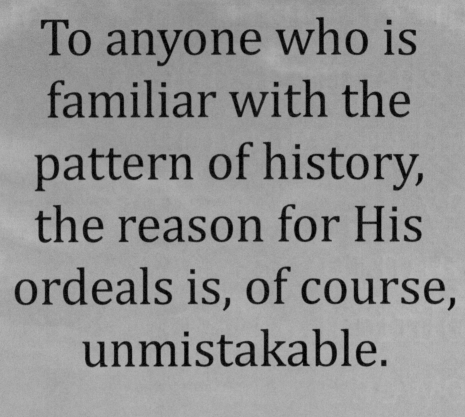

To anyone who is familiar with the pattern of history, the reason for His ordeals is, of course, unmistakable.

The appearance of a
prophetic figure

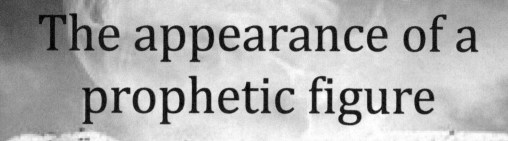

in the
world has invariably
given rise to ferocious
opposition from
wielders of power.

In the lives of these transcendent Beings one finds sacrifice, heroism, and deeds exemplifying Their words.

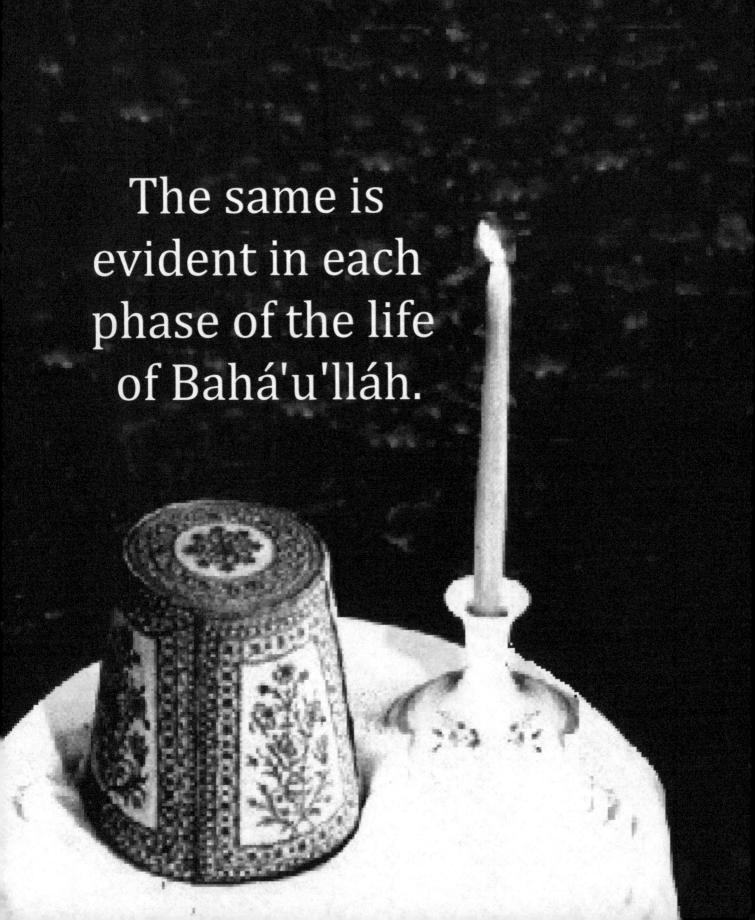

The same is evident in each phase of the life of Bahá'u'lláh.

In spite of
every hardship,
He was never
silenced.

His words
retained their
compelling potency.

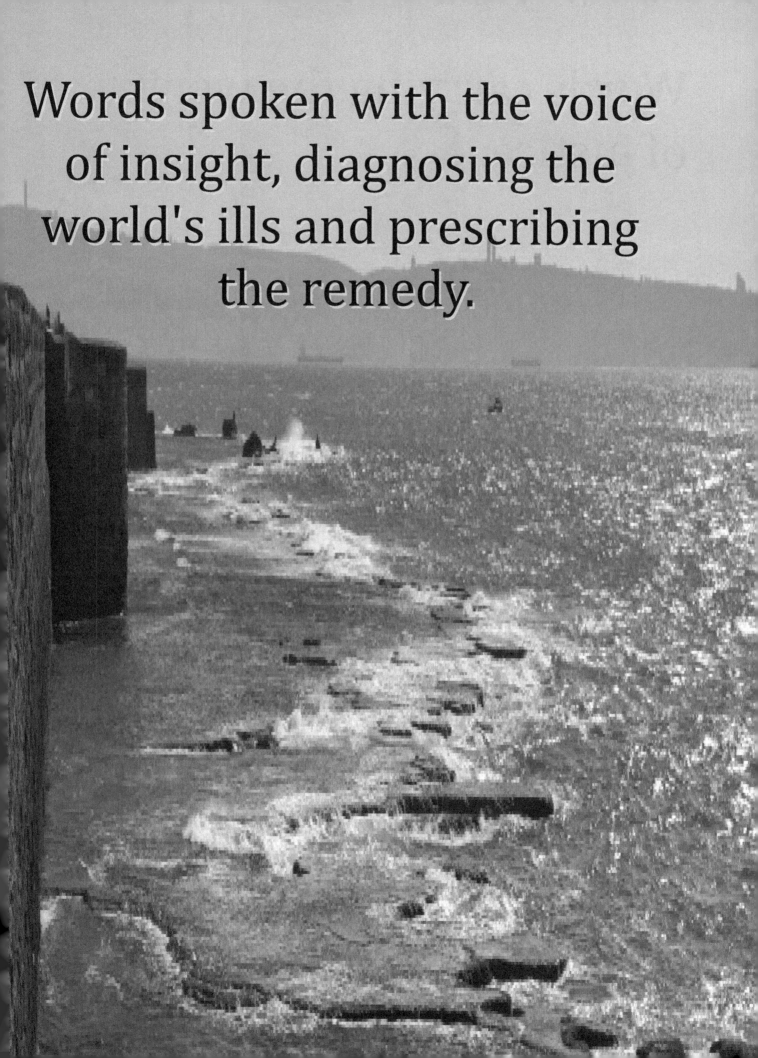

Words spoken with the voice of insight, diagnosing the world's ills and prescribing the remedy.

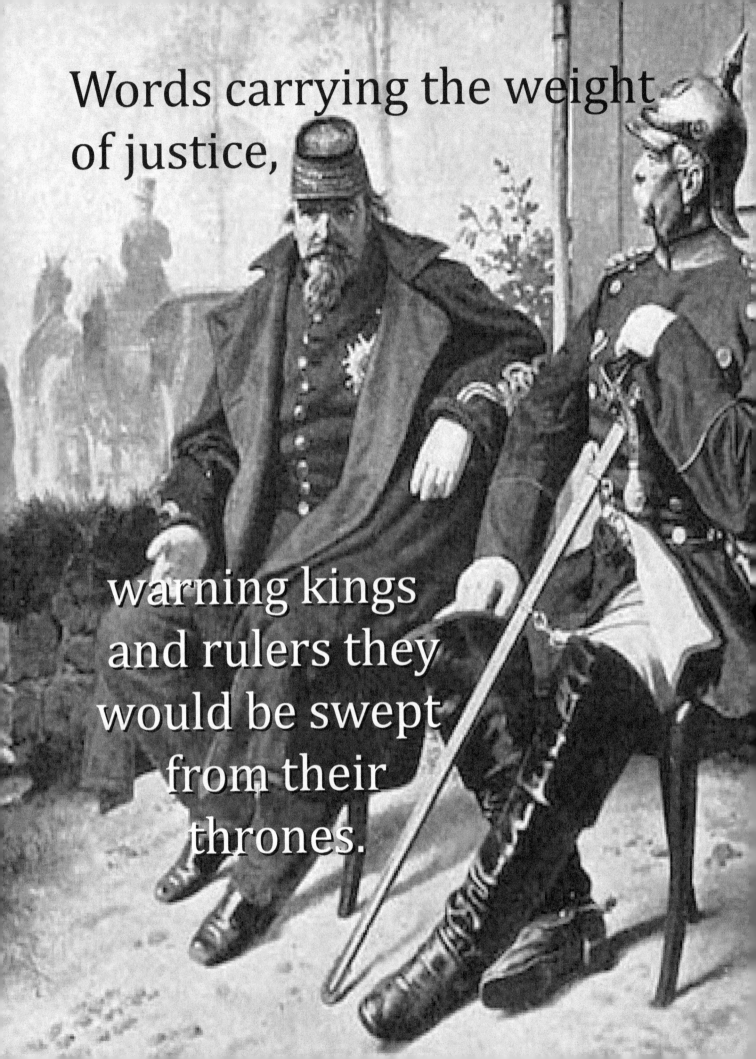

Words carrying the weight of justice,

warning kings and rulers they would be swept from their thrones.

Words leaving one's soul uplifted, awed, transformed and

determined to free itself from the thorns and brambles of self-interest.

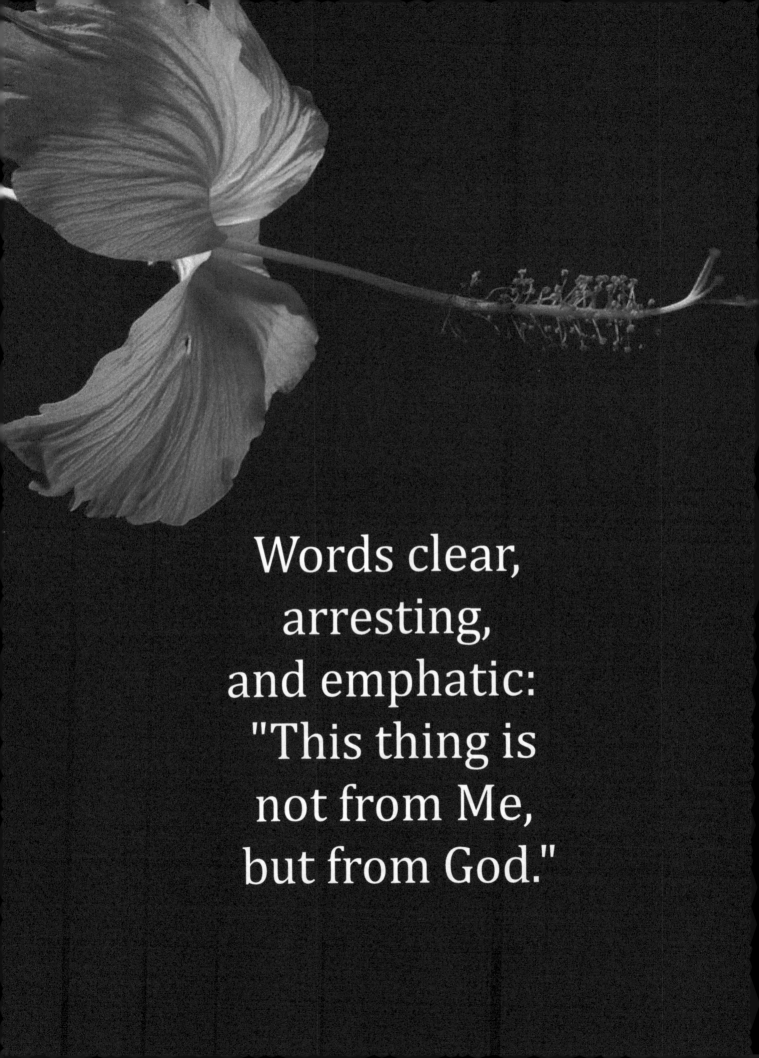

Words clear,
arresting,
and emphatic:
"This thing is
not from Me,
but from God."

Might one not ask, in considering such a life:

If this be not from God, what can be pointed to that is?

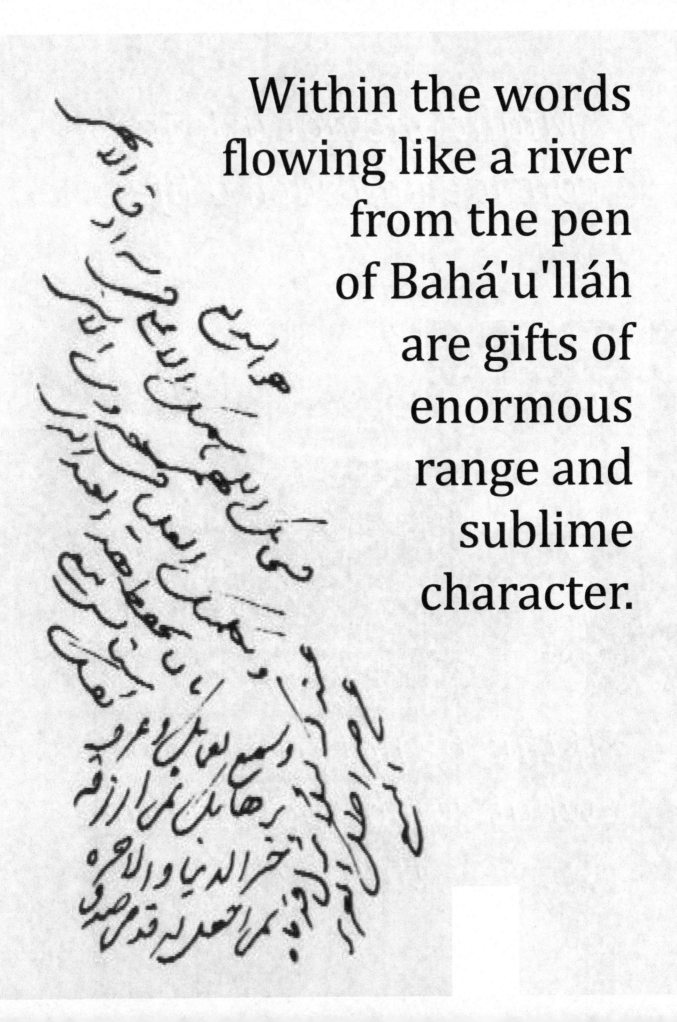

Within the words flowing like a river from the pen of Bahá'u'lláh are gifts of enormous range and sublime character.

One who encounters His Revelation responds first to prayers of surpassing beauty

Prayers
which satisfy the
soul's longing
to befittingly
worship its
Maker.

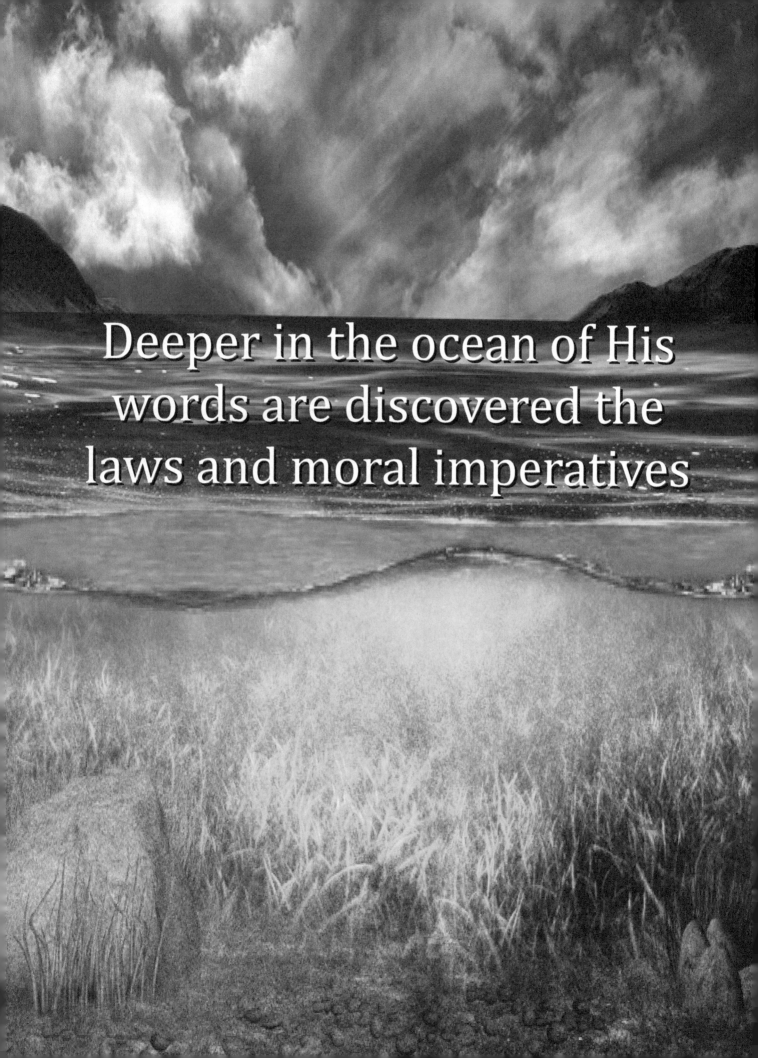

Deeper in the ocean of His words are discovered the laws and moral imperatives

to
liberate
the human
spirit
from
the
tyranny
of worldly
instincts
unworthy of its
true calling.

Here are found
enduring ideals

in whose light parents may
raise children, not simply in
their own likeness, but with
aspirations more exalted.

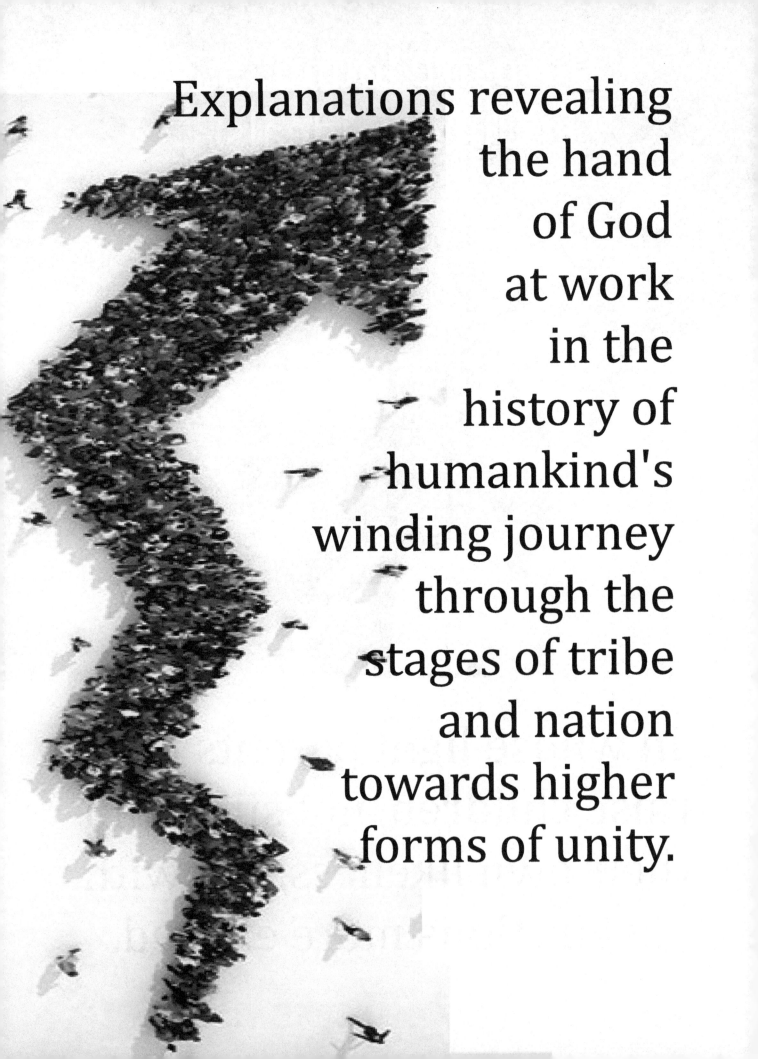

Explanations revealing the hand of God at work in the history of humankind's winding journey through the stages of tribe and nation towards higher forms of unity.

The diverse religions of the world are shown to be expressions of a single underlying truth,

related to one
another by a
common
origin, by a
common
purpose:
to
transform
humanity's
inner life
and
outer
conditions

Bahá'u'lláh's teachings testify to the nobility of the human spirit.

The society He envisions is one worthy of nobility founded on principles which guard and reinforce it.

The oneness of the human
family He places at the
core of collective life.

The equality of
women and men
He unequivocally asserts.

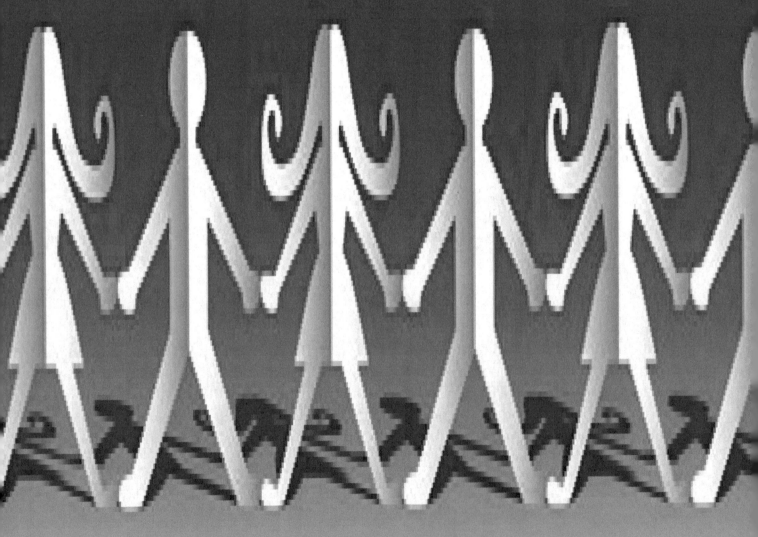

He reconciles
the seemingly
counteracting forces
of our own age:

science and
religion,

unity and diversity,

freedom
and order,

individual
rights
and
social
responsibilities

His
greatest
gift is
justice,

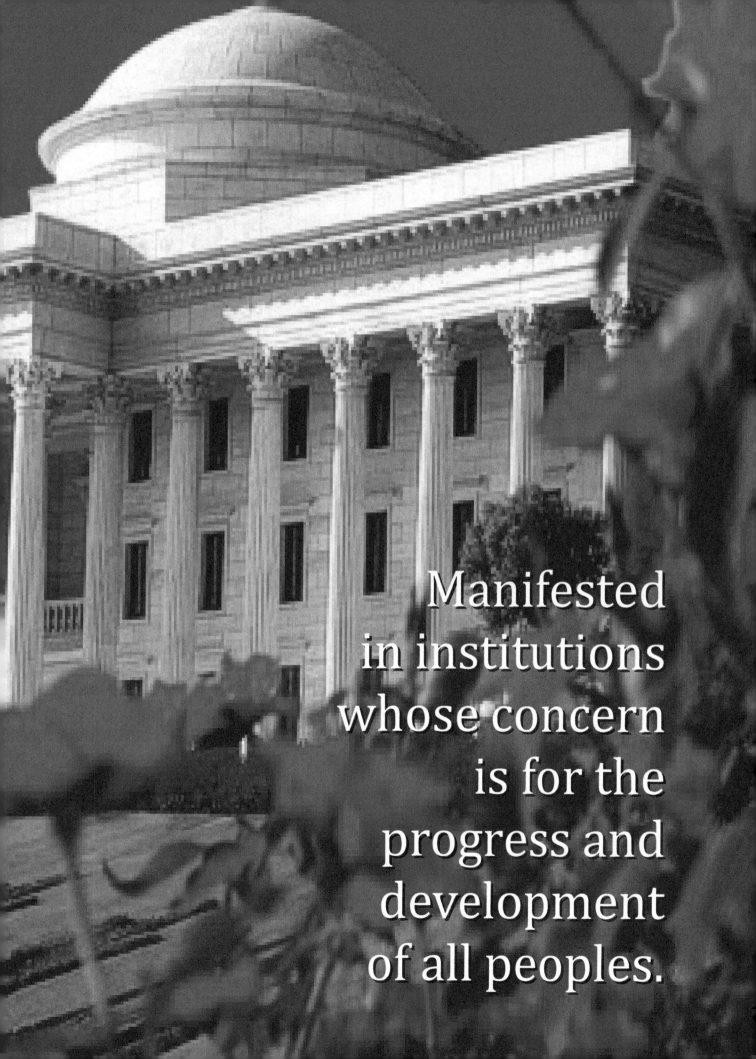

Manifested
in institutions
whose concern
is for the
progress and
development
of all peoples.

Bahá'u'lláh "blotted out from the pages of God's holy Book whatsoever hath been the cause of strife, of malice and mischief amongst the children of men

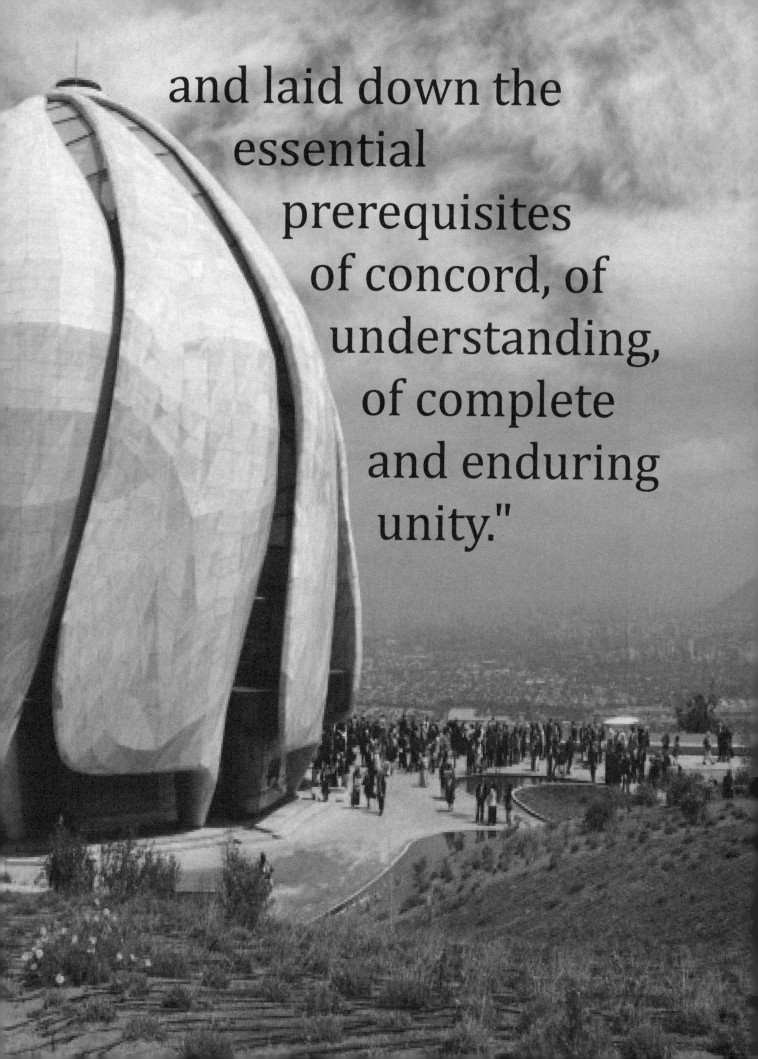

and laid down the essential prerequisites of concord, of understanding, of complete and enduring unity."

*Might one not ask,
what would be a
befitting response
to such gifts?*

"It is the duty of every seeker to bestir himself and strive to attain the shores of this ocean," Bahá'u'lláh answers.

Throughout history,
the spiritual teachings
brought by successive
Messengers
have been

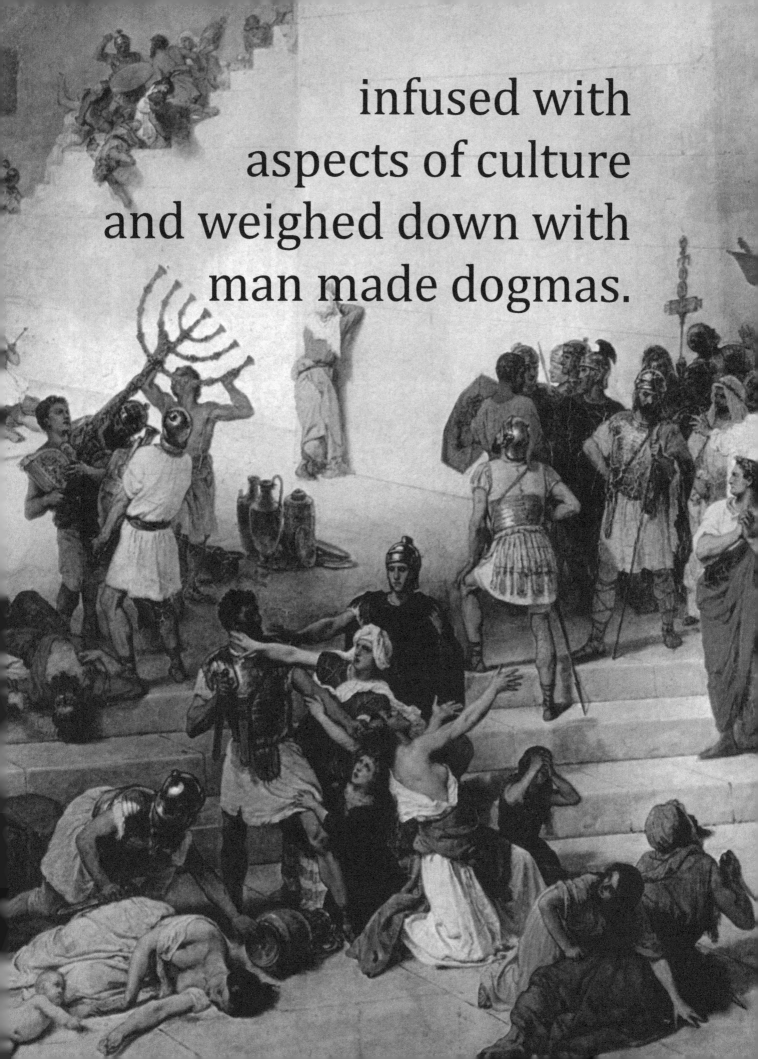

infused with
aspects of culture
and weighed down with
man made dogmas.

But look past these additions and it becomes clear the original teachings are the source of universal values.

through which diverse
peoples have found
common cause

and
which
have molded
humanity's moral
consciousness.

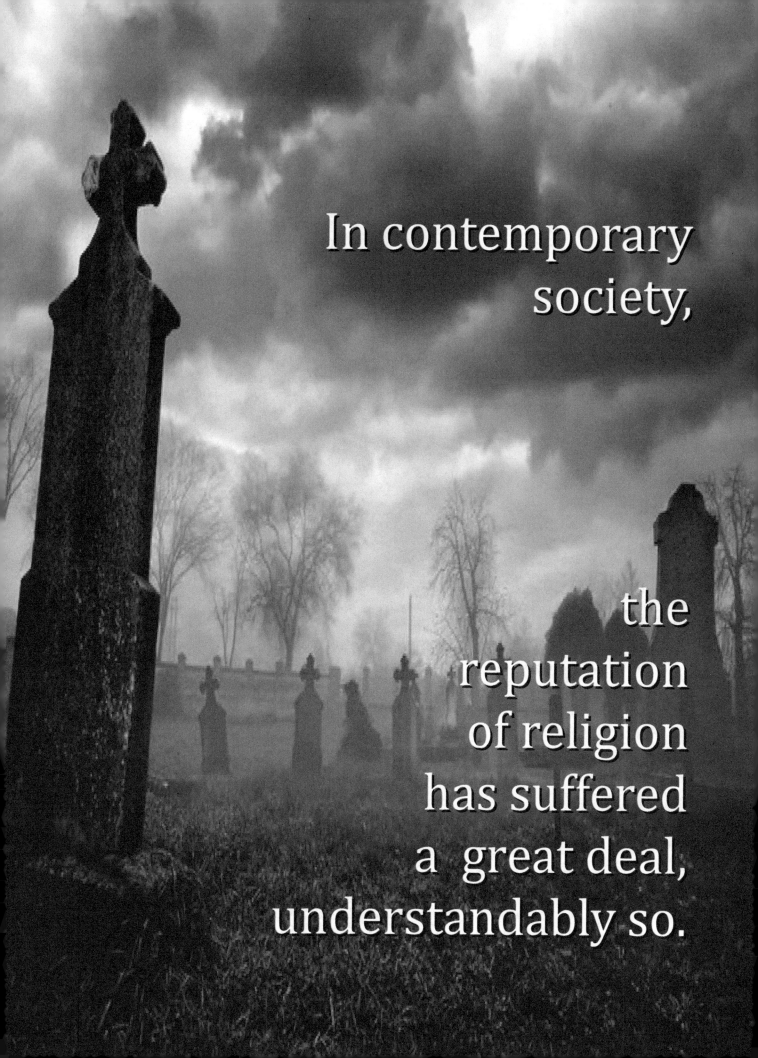

In contemporary society, the reputation of religion has suffered a great deal, understandably so.

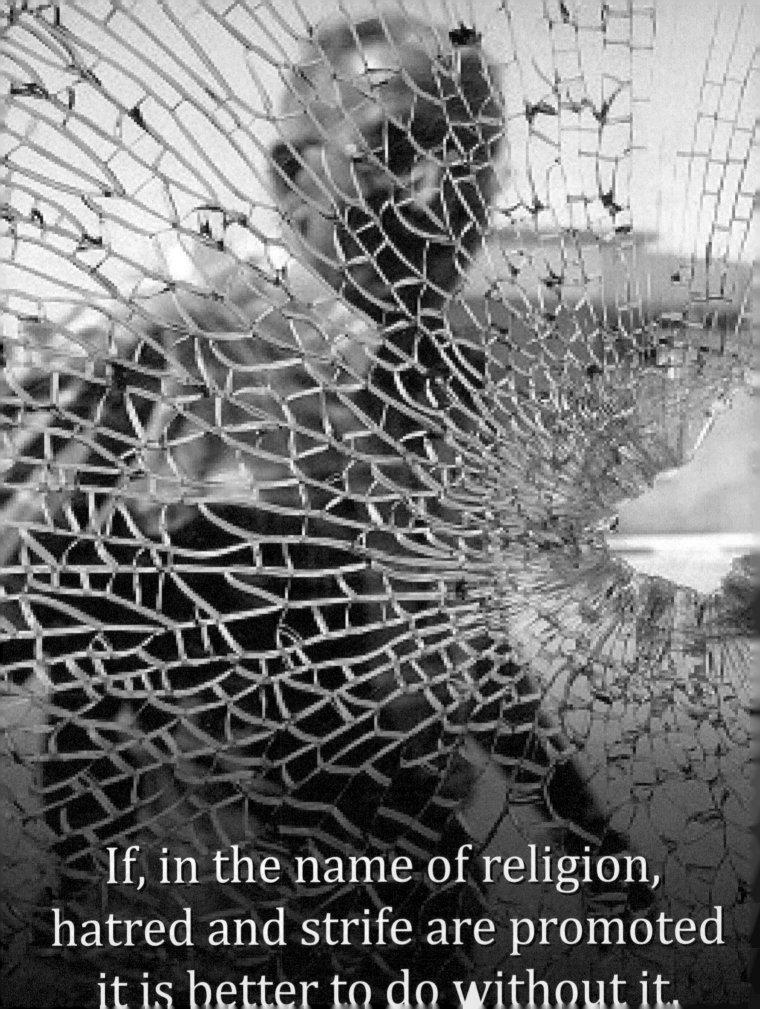

If, in the name of religion,
hatred and strife are promoted
it is better to do without it.

However, true religion is known by its fruits.

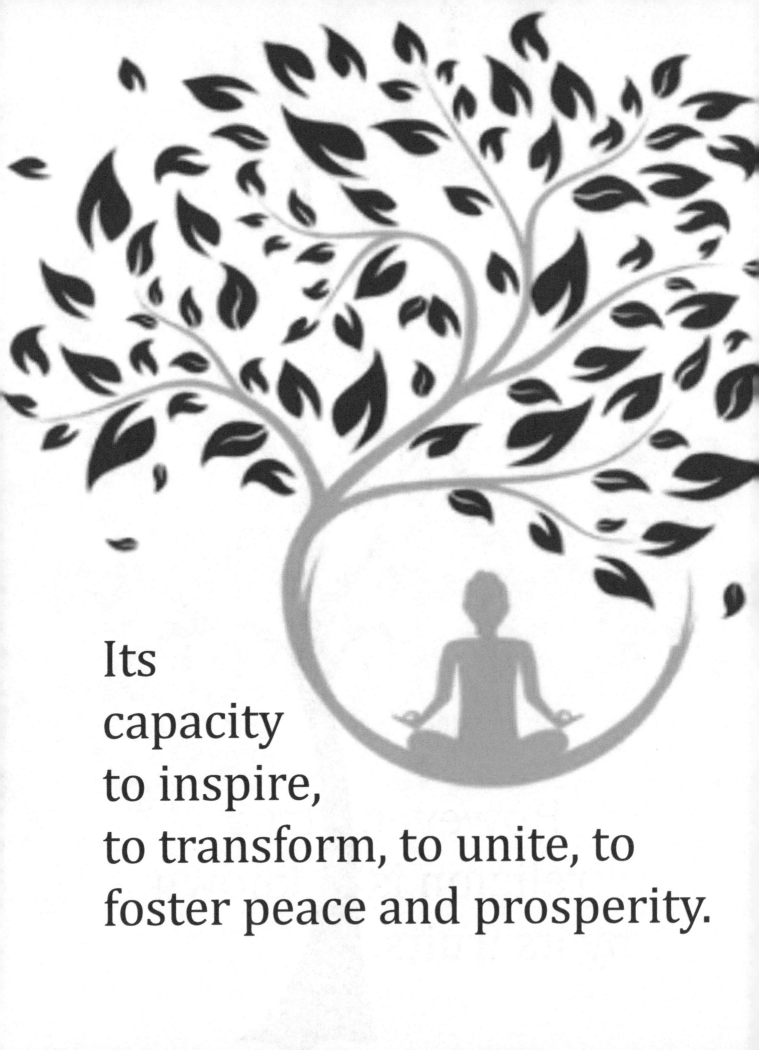

Its
capacity
to inspire,
to transform, to unite, to
foster peace and prosperity.

It is in harmony with rational thought and is essential to social progress.

By utilizing the
discipline of acting
in the light of reflection,

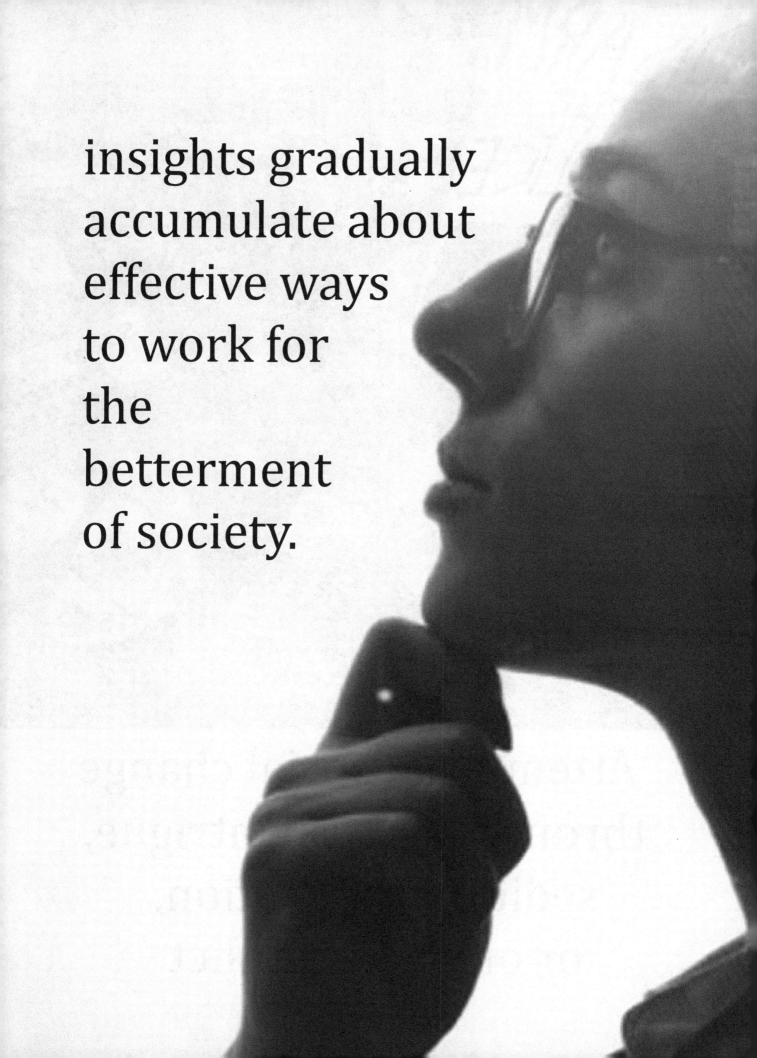

insights gradually
accumulate about
effective ways
to work for
the
betterment
of society.

Attempts at social change
through political intrigue,
sedition, vilification,
or outright conflict

are condemned by Bahá'u'lláh, for they merely perpetuate cycles of struggle while lasting solutions continue to elude.

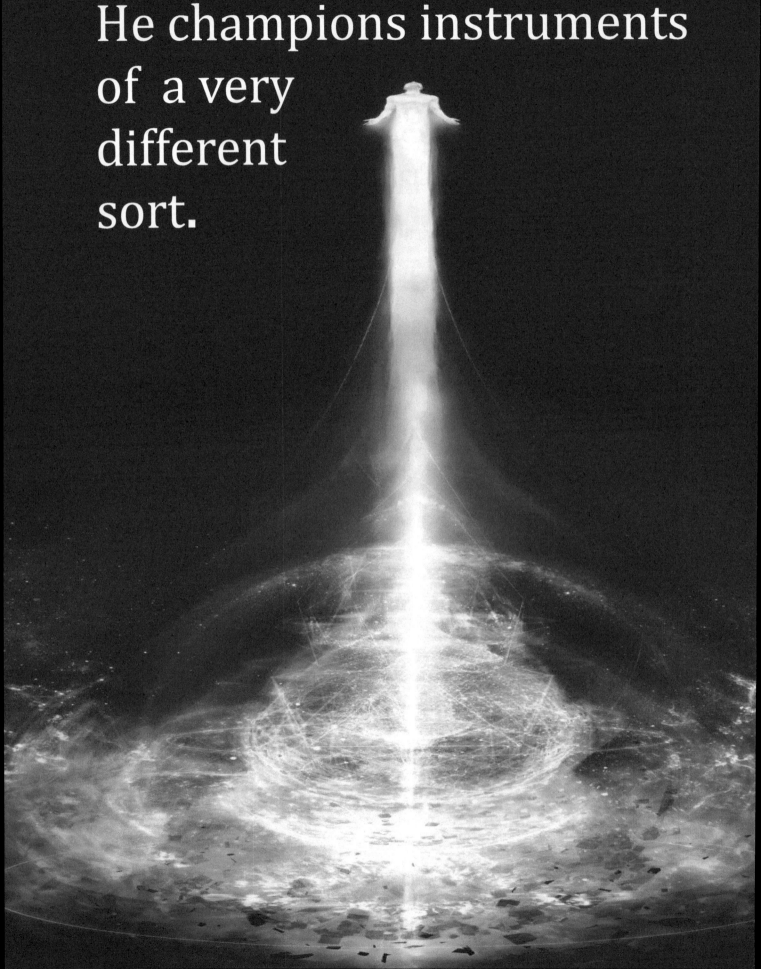

He champions instruments of a very different sort.

He calls
for good
deeds,
kind
words
and
upright
conduct.

He enjoins
service to others
and collaborative
action.

He summons every
member of the human
race to the task of
constructing a

world civilization founded
on the divine teachings.

Might one not ask, in contemplating the breadth of His vision, upon what foundation shall humanity realistically build hope for the future, if not this?

In every land, those who have been attracted to the message of Bahá'u'lláh,

and are
committed
to His vision,

are systematically learning
how to give effect
to His teachings.

Cohorts of youth are becoming ever more conscious of their spiritual identity

and are directing their energies towards the advancement of their societies

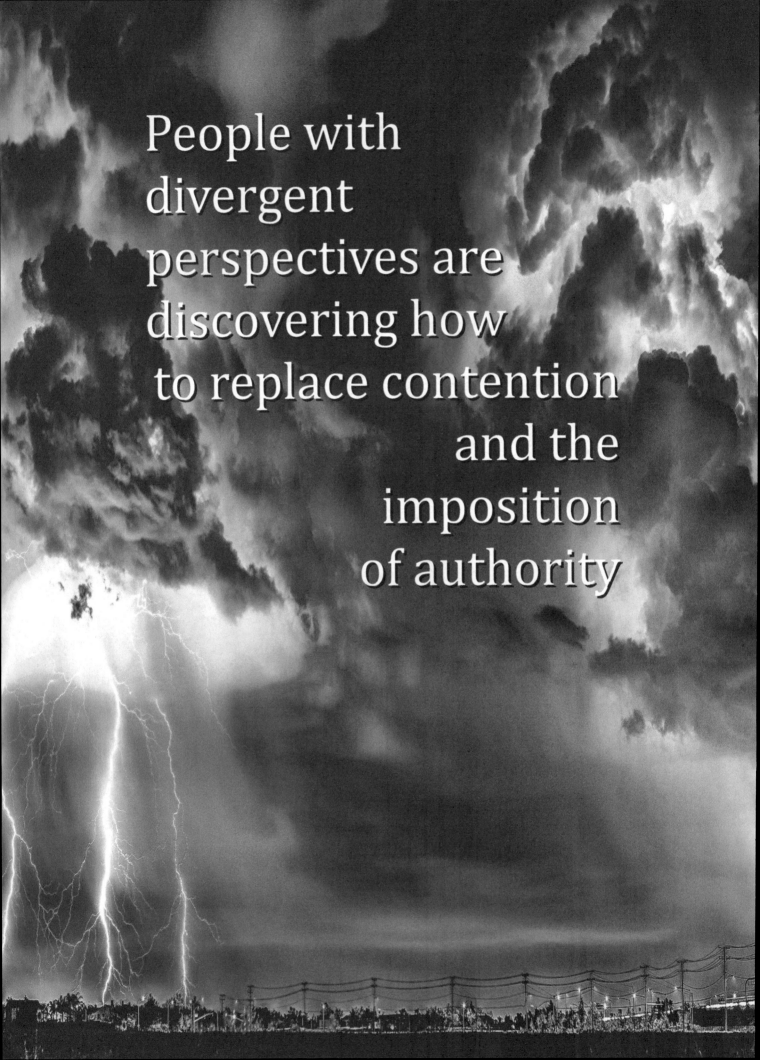

People with divergent perspectives are discovering how to replace contention and the imposition of authority

with consultation and the collective search for solutions.

From every race, religion,
nationality and class,
so many are uniting around
a vision of humanity
as one people and
the earth as one country.

Many who have long suffered
are finding their voice

and becoming
protagonists of their
own development,
resourceful and resilient.

From cities, towns, villages,
and neighborhoods are arising
institutions, communities,
and individuals dedicated
to laboring together

about effective ways to work
for the betterment
of society.

for the emergence of a united
and prospering world

deserved
to be called the
Kingdom of God
on earth.

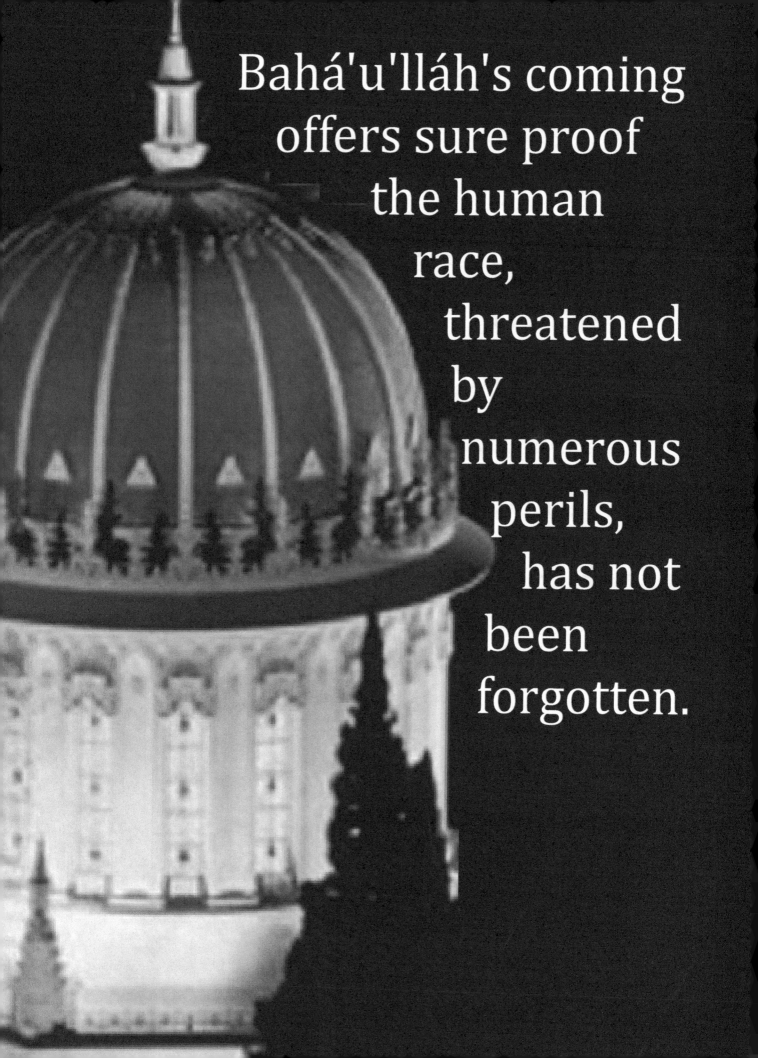

Bahá'u'lláh's coming offers sure proof the human race, threatened by numerous perils, has not been forgotten.

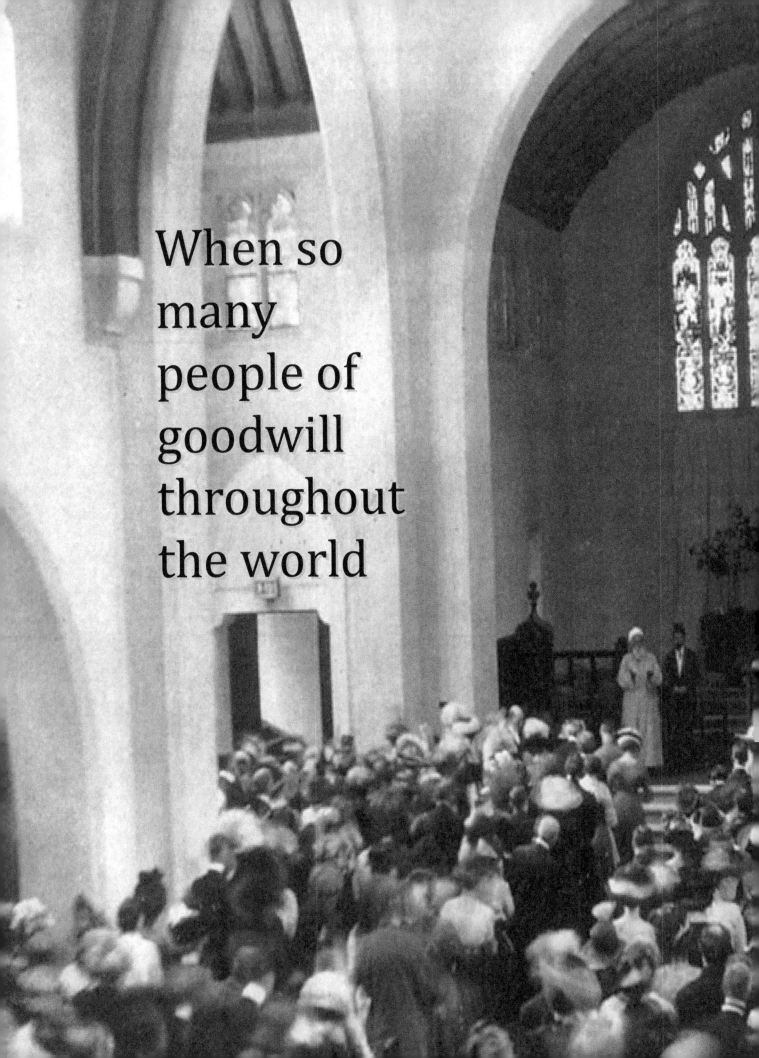

When so
many
people of
goodwill
throughout
the world

have for so long beseeched God for an answer to the problems which beset them in their common homeland,

is it so surprising He should have answered their prayer?

The many who are part of Bahá'u'lláh's enterprise are reaching out to those around them with a simple invitation:

Leonid Afremov

Seize this opportunity to find out who He was and what He represents.

Biblography

The National Spiritual Assembly of the Bahá'ís of the United States, Letter to the American Bahá'í community, February 25, 2017

The Universal House of Justice, A Celebration of the Glory of God, October 2017

Shoghi Effendi, The Promised Day is Come
Shoghi Effendi, The World Order of Bahá'u'lláh

BahaiTeachings.org, "Building a Culture of Oneness" by Robert Atkinson, May 23, 2017